Aurora Presents
DON BLUTH PRODUCTIONS'

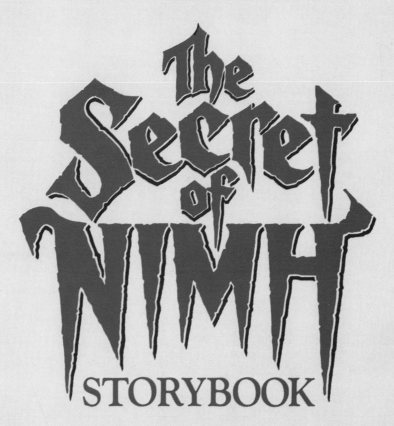

The Secret of NIMH

STORYBOOK

Adapted by Seymour Reit
Illustrated with original artwork from the
motion picture by Don Bluth Productions

Golden Press • New York
Western Publishing Company, Inc., Racine, Wisconsin

Based upon the film THE SECRET OF NIMH, which is based upon
the book MRS. FRISBY AND THE RATS OF NIMH by Robert C. O'Brien.

Spring was coming.

All the animals and birds and insects on the Fitzgibbons farm were getting ready for the new season.

But one of the animals, a field mouse named Mrs. Jonathan Brisby, had other things on her mind. She was a poor widow with four small children, and one of them, Timmy, was very sick.

So Mrs. Brisby was hurrying to see Mr. Ages, a wise medicine mouse who lived nearby.

She found him in his laboratory and told him Timmy's symptoms. Mr. Ages frowned.

"I'm afraid your son has pneumonia," he said. "Keep him home in bed. He can't go outside for at least three weeks."

"Three weeks!" cried Mrs. Brisby. "But Moving Day is almost here! We *must* move before the farmer's plow comes and wrecks our home!"

"I don't care about plows and moving days," said Mr. Ages, grinding and mixing powders with his mortar and pestle. "The boy must stay in bed. Here's some medicine. It will bring down his fever."

On her way home, Mrs. Brisby met a friendly, clumsy crow named Jeremy, who was collecting pieces of string. "I'm saving string to build me a nest for two," he explained. "Now all I need is Miss Right!"

But Jeremy was better at collecting trouble than collecting string, and he got all tangled up. He began to flap his wings and thrash about.

"Ssh," warned Mrs. Brisby as she tried to untangle the string. "If you keep making all that noise Dragon will hear you. He's Farmer Fitzgibbons's cat, and he's very mean!"

Jeremy laughed. "Don't worry," he said. "If there were a cat nearby I'd start sneezing. I'm a-a-*choo!* allergic to ca-ca-*choo!*"

Jeremy turned around—and sneezed right into the face of Dragon. Hissing and yowling, the cat pounced at him.

"Help! Don't panic!" screamed Jeremy, his wings flapping wildly.

Just in time, Mrs. Brisby loosened the last string. Jeremy flew off into a treetop.

Now Dragon went after Mrs. Brisby. He swiped at her, his long, sharp claws ready to grab her. She ducked. He came at her again—and this time he almost got her.

Suddenly Jeremy swooped down. A string still dangled from his leg. "Quick!" he yelled to Mrs. Brisby. "Grab the string!" Mrs. Brisby did, and Jeremy carried her to safety.

When the two finally had a chance to catch their breath, Mrs. Brisby realized she had lost Timmy's medicine.

"Oh, no!" she sobbed. "What will I do now?"

"Hey," said Jeremy, "I'm okay! Wasn't I great? Please don't cry. I hate to see a woman cry. By the way, you dropped this back there."

He handed her the envelope containing the medicine.

"That's it!" cried Mrs. Brisby. "Oh, thank you! You found it!"

"I did? I mean, I did!" said Jeremy. Bewildered but pleased, he escorted Mrs. Brisby home.

As Mrs. Brisby was giving Timmy his medicine, Auntie Shrew, their neighbor, rushed in.

"The frost is off the ground!" she cried. "Fitzgibbons will be starting up his tractor any time now, and he'll come smack through here with that big plow. Quick—leave before it's too late!"

"We *can't* leave," said Mrs. Brisby, beginning to cry. "I mustn't move Timmy—he's too sick. Oh, what are we going to do?"

"Don't worry, dear," said Auntie Shrew. "We'll think of something." Then she smiled. "The Great Owl! *He'll* know what to do. You must go see him."

Mrs. Brisby shuddered. "That's t-too dangerous! Owls *eat* mice."

"Have courage," said Auntie Shrew. "Remember, you're fighting for Timmy's life."

Mrs. Brisby realized Auntie Shrew was right. So that evening she got
Jeremy to fly her to the Great Owl's lair in the forest. It was a frightening ride
for Mrs. Brisby, but she held tight and got there safely.

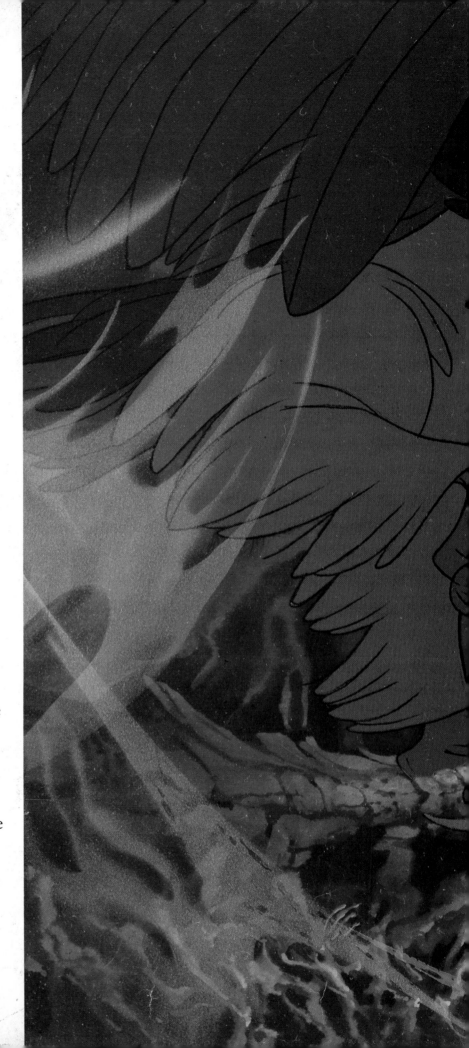

The Great Owl lived in an
ancient, rotting tree. While
Jeremy waited outside, tiny
Mrs. Brisby crept into the
darkness. She scampered past
bats and bones, past cobwebs
and crawly things. She was
more frightened than she had
ever been before.

Suddenly the Great Owl
loomed over her!

His huge eyes glowed. His
talons looked sharp as knives.

"Why have you come?" he
asked, his thunderous voice
echoing in the darkness.

"Forgive me for disturbing
you," said Mrs. Brisby, "but my
son's life is in great danger. The
plow has come early to the
field, and—"

The owl interrupted her.
"Move your family. . . . Move
to a place where you will be safe
from the plow."

"But Timothy has pneumonia," said Mrs. Brisby. "He can't get out of bed. There must be another way."

The Great Owl frowned. "There *is* no other way, Mrs. . . . ?"

"Mrs. Brisby," the little mouse said.

The owl leaned forward. "Mrs. Jonathan Brisby?" he asked.

"Yes," said Mrs. Brisby. "Why?"

"Your husband was not unknown in these woods," replied the owl. "So I will say this: *There is a way. Go to the rats. The ones under the rosebush near the farmhouse. Ask for Nicodemus.*"

"But how can a few rats help me?" asked Mrs. Brisby.

"They have ways," rumbled the owl. "Tell them to move your house . . . to the lee of the big stone."

Then the Great Owl stepped past Mrs. Brisby and, with a whoosh and a flurry, flew out into the night sky.

Mrs. Brisby was alone. She crept back out of the tree.

"What did he say, Mizz Brizz?" asked Jeremy.

"He said I must go to the rats and tell them to move my house to the lee of the stone. . . ."

It was all very strange, thought Mrs. Brisby. But when the Great Owl told you to do something, you did it.

Early the next morning, Mrs. Brisby asked Jeremy to stay with the children. Then she scurried off to the rats' hiding place.

She searched all around the rosebush. At last she found a hidden entrance. Timidly, she stepped inside.

The secret world of the rats was the most mysterious place Mrs. Brisby had ever seen. Strange stone carvings surrounded her, and lights flashed from every direction. She was looking around in wonder when a giant guard rat leaped out and chased her away from the entrance.

Mrs. Brisby was frightened. But just in time a friend came along—none other than Mr. Ages!

"What are you doing here?" the old mouse asked.

"The Great Owl told me to come," Mrs. Brisby replied.

"The Great Owl!" he muttered. "Well, well! Come along, then. I'll take you to Nicodemus."

Mr. Ages led Mrs. Brisby down . . . down . . . down into the domain of the mysterious rats of NIMH.

They came to a vast hall that was all a-twinkle with Christmas-tree lights. Under their feet lay a beautiful carpet.

Justin, the Captain of the Guard, welcomed them.

"These lights are beautiful!" exclaimed Mrs. Brisby.

"Yes, ma'am," Justin replied. "We've had electricity for years. But our shame is that we steal it."

"You steal it?" asked Mrs. Brisby.

Justin nodded sadly. "We've been taking power from Farmer Fitzgibbons. We also take his grain and water. But soon this stealing will stop. In three weeks, the rats of NIMH are moving to Thorn Valley. There we will grow our *own* food, dig our *own* wells, and build our *own* generators."

"A few of the rats don't want to go," said Mr. Ages. "They would rather stay here and keep on stealing. But Nicodemus has made up his mind. Come along, Mrs. Brisby—it's time for you to meet him." He and Justin led her to an underwater elevator that took them to Nicodemus's quarters.

Nicodemus was the wise old leader of the rats. Crowded bookshelves covered the walls of his candlelit rooms. Even the tables were piled high with thick, dusty books.

"Your husband," he said to Mrs. Brisby, "was a great friend of the rats of NIMH. Without his help, we could not have come here, nor stayed so long. It was while helping us that Jonathan met his end."

"Jonathan never told me about you," said Mrs. Brisby.

"Then it is time you knew," said Nicodemus.

"In the beginning," said Nicodemus, "we were ordinary street rats. We stole our daily bread and lived off the work of men. After all, that has always been the way of rats. . . .

"One day we were captured and sent to a place called NIMH. We were thrown into tiny cages, where scientists injected chemicals into us with sharp needles and used us for experiments. . . .

"No doubt the scientists had reasons. But for us it was cruel and painful. We hated the bare little cages. We hated being prisoners. We yearned to be free and happy again. . . .

"Then, to our surprise, we found that the injections were making us very intelligent. We found that we could read. We kept all this secret from our jailers. . . .

"Late one night we opened our cages and escaped from the laboratory by crawling through the ventilating system. Two mice escaped with us. One was Mr. Ages. The other was your husband. It was Jonathan who saved us at the last minute. He managed to open a locked door on the roof so we could get away. . . .

"He continued to help us here on the farm. When we had to be out in the open, he would sneak into the farmhouse and drug Dragon, the cat, so we could work safely. He was killed on one of those missions. Jonathan died a hero, Mrs. Brisby."

"I had no idea . . . " Mrs. Brisby whispered.

"I have a gift for you," said Nicodemus. "Your husband wanted you to have this." He gave her a small oval stone on a chain. It sparkled softly in her hand.

Mrs. Brisby turned the stone over and read the words on the back: *You can unlock any door if you only have the key.*

"It's beautiful," she gasped.

Nicodemus nodded. "The stone sleeps. But it will glow bright red with magic life when it is worn by one with a courageous heart."

"A courageous heart?" asked Mrs. Brisby.

"Yes," said Nicodemus. *"Courage of the heart is very rare. The stone has a power when it's there."* He stood up. "And now we must make plans for moving your house."

That night it started to rain. Quickly and quietly, the rats of NIMH got ready to move Mrs. Brisby's cinder-block house. The rats planned to lift the house with their ropes and pulleys and move it to the lee of the stone.

Soon all was ready. Off went the rats in the pouring rain.

Mrs. Brisby was part of the plan, too. She was going to put sleeping powder in the cat's food. "Jonathan would have wanted me to do my share," she said.

With Justin at her side, Mrs. Brisby waited under the farmhouse kitchen floor. Her heart was pounding. At just the right moment, she darted out and dropped the powder into Dragon's dish.

But she wasn't fast enough. Before she could scurry away—CLANG!—a metal colander came down over her. She was caught by the farmer's little boy.

He locked her in an old birdcage. She struggled to get out but cut herself. Holding her arm, she waited for the bleeding to stop.

"I'll come back," Justin whispered to himself. "We have to get the house moved first!" Quickly, he crawled back out from under the farmhouse.

Meanwhile, the rats were busy with their ropes and pulleys, slowly moving Mrs. Brisby's house.

But there were troublemakers in the group—the rats who didn't want to move to Thorn Valley. Their leader, Jenner, decided this would be a perfect time to do away with Nicodemus.

"Then *I'll* be leader of all the rats," Jenner said to his friend Sullivan, "and I can call off the foolish move to Thorn Valley."

Jenner and Sullivan waited and watched as the others strained and pulled at the ropes.

"Now!" said Jenner suddenly. "Nicodemus is in exactly the right position. Cut the line, Sullivan."

But Sullivan held back. "I can't do it," he said. "It's murder. I want no part of murder."

Jenner was enraged. "Fool!" he cried, stabbing Sullivan. As Sullivan lay wounded, Jenner cut the main line himself.

Down came everything with a thundering crash—house, ropes, pulleys, and poles.

A heavy pole landed right on Nicodemus. Justin and the others struggled to pull him out from under it. But by the time they freed him, Nicodemus was dead.

"Now," shouted Jenner, "I'm the leader of the rats of NIMH!"

Meanwhile, Mrs. Brisby had been feverishly trying to get out of the birdcage. By jumping into the water feeder and squeezing through a tiny opening behind it, she had at last managed to escape.

Now, out of breath, she came running up to the rats. "What's happening?" she cried. "Where are my children? Are they all right?"

Mr. Ages came forward and said, "Your children are safe inside your house. But our beloved leader, Nicodemus, is dead."

"Oh, no," said Mrs. Brisby. "Oh, I'm so sorry." She hugged Mr. Ages in sympathy. Then, breaking the somber mood, she said, "But I'm afraid you're all in great danger! While I was trapped in the cage, I heard the farmer talking on the telephone. The people from NIMH have found out where you are. They're coming in the morning to bulldoze your rosebush and kill you!"

Jenner jumped up. "That's a lie!" he snarled. "You're making it up!"

"You must believe me," cried Mrs. Brisby. "Leave for Thorn Valley right away! Run before you're all killed!"

Suddenly Jenner spied the magic stone hanging from Mrs. Brisby's neck.

"That amulet! I must have it!" he cried. "I'm the new leader—it should be mine!"

He grabbed at Mrs. Brisby—but Justin stopped him. "Now I see it all," Justin said. "*You* are to blame for Nicodemus's death!"

Drawing his sword, Jenner turned on Justin. "You won't stand in my way, either!" he growled.

A fierce battle began.

Jenner swung with his sharp, heavy sword. Justin ducked. Jenner swung again. He hit Justin in the shoulder, knocking him to the ground.

Now Jenner moved toward Mrs. Brisby. His sword just missed her but caught her cape, and she stumbled and fell. Paralyzed by fear, she saw Jenner raise his sword again.

Justin leaped between them. This time the fight was quick. With a few swift, skillful thrusts of his sword, Justin wounded Jenner badly. As the villain hobbled away, Justin dropped his sword and turned to the other rats. "We leave for Thorn Valley tonight!" he said.

Jenner whirled around. "No you won't!" he screamed, lunging at Justin from behind.

Suddenly something stirred in the shadows. Sullivan, gasping and barely alive, threw his knife at Jenner's back and then fell dead. The knife hit Jenner squarely between the shoulders, killing him instantly.

The rats were glad to see the last of Jenner. They all turned and looked at Mrs. Brisby's house, lying on its side in the muddy field.

"Mommy," the children called from inside, "are we moved yet?"

"Soon, dears," replied Mrs. Brisby. Then she gasped. The house was slowly sinking in the mud!

The rats grabbed the ropes and tried to hold the house. But there was little they could do without their pulleys and poles, which now lay broken and tangled among the cut line.

"My children!" screamed Mrs. Brisby, leaping to the top of the house. She clung to the house desperately, as if somehow she could keep it from going down.

But the mud rose around her, and the house sank lower and lower. Finally it—and Mrs. Brisby—disappeared.

A moment later Mrs. Brisby struggled to the surface. "My children," she gasped as Justin pulled her from the mud. "Please, you must help me save my children!"

"We will," said Justin. "I promise." Then he noticed something—the amulet was gone from Mrs. Brisby's neck. He started to tell her, but Mrs. Brisby was gazing past him at something that held her transfixed. Justin turned to look.

Rising out of the mud, glowing fiery red, the amulet was floating toward Mrs. Brisby. Justin and the others stepped back, awestruck, as Nicodemus's face appeared in the amulet and spoke to Mrs. Brisby.

"Courage of the heart is very rare.

The stone has a power when it's there."

Mrs. Brisby knew now what she had to do.

Mrs. Brisby took the glowing stone in her hand. Its searing heat burned her fingers, but she did not let go. Thinking only of her children, she put the fiery amulet around her neck. Its energy surged through her until she herself glowed red with its power.

Mrs. Brisby picked up the one rope that remained above the surface of the mud. As soon as she touched it, the rope took on a magical glow. Even the mud began to glimmer and bubble, churning faster and faster, until . . . in a blinding burst of light, the house emerged from the sinkhole and began to rise.

Up, up it came, slowly, steadily, up from the choking mud.

Up, up, shining and gleaming, while Mrs. Brisby held the glowing rope in her hands.

Guided by Mrs. Brisby and the power of the amulet, the house glided through the air and settled itself gently on the lee side of the big stone.

Mrs. Brisby's family and home were safe from the farmer's plow at last.

The next morning, before sunrise, the rats left for Thorn Valley. Mrs. Brisby gave Justin the magic stone. "You'll need it where you're going," she said.

Soon Jeremy came flapping by, with lots of string to help move Mrs. Brisby's house.

"Thank you," she said. "We're already moved."

"Great, Mizz Brizz!" said Jeremy. "I can use this dandy string for my new love nest. . . . But what does a guy like me need with a love nest, anyway?"

As he turned to go, something suddenly crashed into him.

"Hey!" cried Jeremy. "What the—" Then he blinked. There before him, tangled in yards of brightly colored string, was the loveliest, clumsiest lady crow he had ever seen.

"Oh, pardon me," she said, giggling shyly as she tried to untangle herself.

Jeremy could hardly contain himself. "Mizz Brizz," he called joyfully, "I found her! It's Miss Right!"

Mrs. Brisby smiled as she and her children watched Jeremy and his new friend fly off together.

When the two crows were out of sight, Timmy turned to his mother and asked, "Do you think our friends the rats will ever come back?"

There was a faraway look in Mrs. Brisby's eyes. "I don't know, dear," she said. "But I do hope that someday . . . we'll see the wonderful rats of NIMH again. . . ."